POEMS

THIRD AGE

AN ANTHOLOGY

WITH CONTRIBUTIONS BY

JANET BLACKBURN
ANNE BROADBENT
EILEEN CHILVERS
DORIS CORTI
JACKIE DARNBROUGH
TONY HARGREAVES
JACKY KENNEDY
RUTH MAWDSLEY
GILLIAN MCHUGH
ANDREW SHEPHARD
JANE WILSON

Published by Hilltop Communications

ISBN: 978-0-9932669-6-6

Contents

Introduction

Poetry means different things to people, but between the covers of this book you are sure to find strings of words which connect with you, challenge you, or encourage you to put pen to paper yourself. The poems in the anthology reflect the work of eleven contributors using different poetic forms. The poets among you may spot the occasional villanelle, cinquain, roundel, or haiku. All were composed with consideration for each word, observation and imagination. Every poem reflects our enthusiasm for the magic that arises when a thought or feeling is successfully shared.

All the poets who have contributed to this anthology are members of Huddersfield U3A (University of the Third Age) and have attended courses run by the published poet, author, and tutor Doris Corti. She has contributed several of her own prize winning poems (see Acknowledgements) and continues to be powered by poetry at a venerable age. The fact that she is willing to share her lifelong love and knowledge of poetry has helped her students develop their own voices and understand the craft of poetry a little better.

Poetry is sometimes better spoken than read. If you read one of these poems and it leaves you mystified, try reading it aloud. The sound may add to the sense. Most of these poems have been read to a variety of groups by their authors, and the collection is arranged like a public reading, starting with one poem to introduce each contributor. This is followed by a chance to get to know each 'voice' better, with two or three poems by each author grouped together. Anthologies provide the perfect opportunity to stimulate the mind by dipping into poetry. Why not start your day by opening the collection at random and reading a poem or two?

Thanks go to Ruth Mawdsley and Janet Blackburn for allowing us to include their art as incidental illustrations, and to Tony Burke for his wonderful cover illustration and design. I am also very grateful to Emma Harding of Hilltop Communications for bringing our ideas to fruition, to Alison Chisholm for her encouragement, and to Andrea Ditchfield for final proof-reading.

Get in touch with us through the U3A if you would like a reading by these poets at your library or local event.

Andrew Shephard

It has been my privilege to lead and encourage these members of the Huddersfield U3A poetry writing group. There are a variety of poems in this book, written in different voices and different styles. Some are in traditional forms and others in free verse. All were composed using imagination, observation, and enthusiasm. Enjoy!

Doris Corti
Poet, author, tutor
Vice President Society of Women Writers and Journalists

Fox in suburbia

He has come defiantly
through firm fences and over shut gate
into the stillness
that lies like a drawn breath over the garden;

he waits, one paw raised
green eyes in demonic mask stare warily
clouds trail over the moon like an eyelid closing,

trim garden corners dissolve, take asymmetrical shapes,
shocked into this new dimension
I feel his tremor, that like an unseen thought
acknowledges my presence:

he moves deliberately,
yet daintily through shrubs, and young acacias,

a manoeuvre of elegance along the earth trail,
fox is a curving shadow.

Doris Corti

Moon

You are watching,
always watching.
Near to me, far from me,
pulling,
in invisible time.

You dominate the dark
with silvered touches,
shaping shadows,
revelations
of myths long ago.

You are the enigma
sent from galaxies far,
waxing and waning
in liquid black night.
Reflection of those
seduced away,
lost in your promised eternity.

Jackie Darnbrough

Lifeboat

As if goaded by
a frothing mouth of swaggering spittle,
the small rescue vessel
flings itself into the swell of a sea
too frightening to conceive.

Life-riskers, life-savers
search a dynamic shifting surface
in the belly of the beast.
Twenty-three call outs daily
cradle thousands to safety.

Courage of the finest,
wrung from hands and hearts
of lifeboat crews,
is given for free,
to the lives of you and me.

Anne Broadbent

Beachcomber

She dragged her bag
behind the rocks
on a bleak Northumberland beach.

She wore a long flowing skirt,
bright yellow blouse
reminiscent of another time.

Standing, gazing at the shore line,
the sea produced its treasures
along the shingle stretch,

shells, shimmering pink
pebbles, pieces of jet
her only income.

Gillian McHugh

The fox

Trunks, blackened by the rain's slant.
Branches hung with tiny baubles.
Softened by winter rain, leaf litter,
and on its soft bed a fox,
motionless,
perfectly camouflaged.

Chickens he slaughtered
were that same rusty colour.
Chickens I'd fed, named
and in return they'd fed me.
Here the culprit,
that followed his instinct.

Trees rise, cathedral like
over the coldness of his
body, perfect in death.
Silence seeps through the wood.

Jacky Kennedy

Season of life

Time passing weaves a complex tapestry
of misty, sepia shades in autumn's glow.
Tender seeds of youth that we wildly sow,
complete their journey to maturity.
Fruits of our lives, now ripen on the tree
of destiny; though planted long ago
were nurtured tenderly, to help them grow,
their bitter sweetness fills our memory.

This season brings rich harvest, then decays.
Contrasts its brocade cloak of golden hue,
with toadstools growing on the rotting roots.
Autumnal sunlight heralds shorter days,
and as we age, we must face the truth
that this year's fallen leaves, feed next year's shoots.

Janet Blackburn

Sunrise

at the break of the day
the horizon ablaze
as the arc of the sun
burns the last of the haze

the veil of high cirrus
turns from white to pure gold
and the sky is deep blue
a treasure to behold

at the edge of the cloud
a colour creation
with fine pastel shades
in wispy formation

some low cloud turns amber
then to peach and pale pink
that lightens to lilac
and is gone in a blink

a new day created
brings the wonder of birth
in this magical place
that is our planet earth

Tony Hargreaves

Favourite season

There are some who say, that spring has sprung
in April or in May, and some say that Christmas
heralds winter, in a casual sort of way.

In winter, some would say, it's in your best interest
to wear woolly hats and gloves, and just in case you
catch a cold or flu, buy medicine or booze.

The ones who say that summer forecasts sun,
have forgotten rain that buckets down, and when
squelching in your shoes at the garden party planned
ahead, if not carefully, might get a fit of blues.

Autumn, I would say, is the very sanest season,
the reason being, I am in my autumn years,
and I know it might sound silly, but I feel free
to wear my thermals, when the weather turns chilly.
I can draw my curtains early, and snuggle up in bed,
with higher tog duvet, and when all is done and said
I'm going to plump for autumn as my favourite season,
willy nilly.

Eileen Chilvers

The bluebell wood

Green velvet-covered limbs rest
on a carpet of azure and amethyst.
Chandelier light spilling out
golden shards, illuminating
figures dancing a quickstep.

Orchestra on the wing, melodic,
worshipping the delights of spring.
Whispering of huge, ancient oaks,
fluttering green foliage, re-birth,
emerging from winter's long gestation.

Tall, strong trunks, feet entrenched
in earth, covered by nodding heads.
Arms reaching to the sky, forming
a haven, an umbrella, a shelter
for all who stay or just pass by.

Sit awhile, listen, these giants
have wisdom, ancient sages.
Breathe in scent, absorb the hues,
let nature's beauty calm the soul,
with more power than human remedy.

Ruth Mawdsley

Ebb and flow

On this jewel strewn beach
held softly by sand and shells,
racing thoughts peak and trough
now pebble smooth,
mind allowed to slip and still
lulled by the ebb and flow of the sea.

Through heavy lidded eyes
limpid liquid sun releases
a myriad of shattered glints
that effervesce, coalesce,
form and fade.
Mind now letting go.

Hypnotic sounds, bleached and soft
are caught on a breeze.
Inner voice reduced to a
shell whispered echo.

Time suspended between the gaps
and waves
and breath
until I have no edges,
dissolved into this moment now.

Jane Wilson

Waiting for spring

A deer scouts the wood fringe where
a laminated notice shouts, 'It's coming!'
Frozen still, every creature waits.
Buds hold tight, not daring to breathe.

Robin in military red -
a thrush rehearses a private song
while rooks conduct reconnaissance
disguised as twig movements.

Snowfall truce.
Hard ground hesitates to liquefy -
no squirrel springs to action,
no mole digs in mutinous excavation.

Tremor in the night -
heavy plant thunder
then landscape plundered
for trenches, drains and aggregate.

Frost delayed the advance.
Now thaw brings war to fields -
hedges ripped, stone walls breached,
outmanoeuvred creatures flee.

'It's coming! Find a new home,'
the posted notice said.
Only one side can win,
and that side, this year, is not Spring.

Andrew Shephard

Party Shoes

Confined in cobwebbed memories
she greets our visits with mild surprise.
Difficult to locate her in that somewhere-other-world.

We offer flowers and sweets,
she reaches out, hands tissue thin.
Her smile is liquid light, her struggles
are with words,

we wait in cloistered quiet,
until the tea-time trolley intervenes.

Then, 'party shoes!' She shouts, as some happy
recollection escapes from her fragile chains.
Something glimpsed she leaves between us.
Puzzled we retrace her past, and ours, search
through her old home. Hunt for clues
that might disclose the secret of her fragmented joy,

discover in boxes of discarded sepia tints
a snapshot soldier image - uniform and marching boots,
beside him - her honeyed youth in chiffon, lace and party
shoes.

Doris Corti

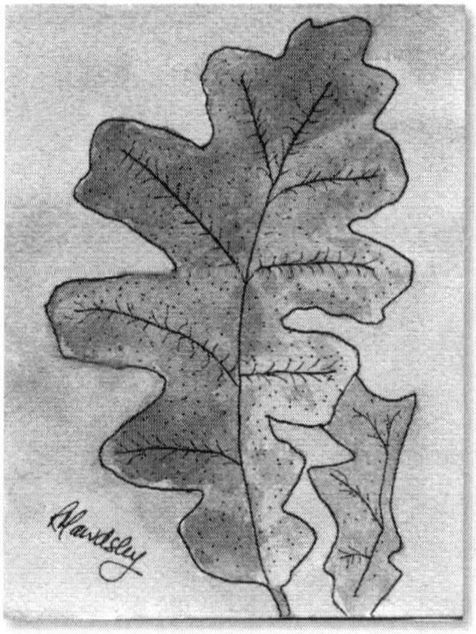

A skylark's song

I kept your shoes and walking boots,
scratched and scuffed like a chopping block; all smoothness lost
in years of walking along earth tracks
and gravel paths.

We'd walk in silence, sometimes see a skylark fly directly
to the sun, the trees ahead 'whispering soft secrets,'
that's what you said.

Our shoes were for ordinary days, but the lacing of boots
were for other times when we found ways through fields and farms,
moors, sunlight and rain.

You took on the job of cleaning boots and shoes. A certain ritual,
first the mud knifed off, a wipe with a damp cloth.
Then polishing, to and fro movement of your hand,
rhythmic flow of brush.

They perch like some emphatic statement on the cupboard floor,
yours and mine where they belong. I thread the laces
through my fingers, almost hear a skylark's song.

Doris Corti

Moonscape

Silver
frosted branches
shimmer in black ice glow
mirrored in dark undulating
moonscape

Delight

In mirrored sheen of raindrops,
silken on flagstones,
morning birdsong through lace leaves.
Cloudscape opening
on a pallid shallow sky,
scent from early dewed grass.

Jackie Darnbrough

Gifts

Seas govern us,
keep us in our place,
know we have no say
if they invade
our breathing space.

Moon roughs them up a little,
pulls them about, in out in,
a rowing machine
building waves with muscle;

at low tide settle into better moods,
chuckles of foam over shingle bear gifts,
tiny stone gems
to wear on our toes.

Anne Broadbent

The heart is

the place to be,
like a kitchen or a library,
the hub of life and activity;
a vast chamber, contained but free,
holding places, people I love
close to me.

Uninvited atrial flutter
thuds unceremoniously;
welcome animals linger
unconditionally.

Why do I stay here?
It beats me...
with its contradiction in terms,
its lifetime guarantee.

Anne Broadbent

Lost

Where is my friend?
No spark.
Medicated to subdue
now she is so blue.
Perhaps a walk in the park
will lift her mood, so dark?
Please, someone give me a clue.

We used to have fun,
lots of larks.
Now she spends her days in bed.
I visit, filled with dread
as she sits
in the dark.
Lost.

Gillian McHugh

Weed or not?

They are here again,
in lawns and borders,
under fences, garden benches
potato trenches.

They grow out of drains,
multiply in country lanes.
Golden heads
love wind and rain
to spread their seed.

They have a certain beauty,
sunny faces, lush green leaves.
Not a weed,
a flower, perhaps?
A dandelion.

Gillian McHugh

Yin and yang

I am black, you are white, I am dark, you are light,
you are dominant, unbending, I am compliant, yielding.
My moon shares the sky with your sun,
darkness needs the moon and stars.

You are a fast flowing river, I am a tranquil pool,
but your river can slow, my pool can ripple.
You motivate and inspire, I create and apply,
you can be me, I can be you, we intertwine.

Two halves that together create wholeness,
each sustains the other, balance and harmony.
My coolness can calm your intense heat,
my rain extinguish your furious fire.

But weights on scales can be uneven,
moon concealed behind clouds,
fire raging too fast to be extinguished,
dense mist obscuring morning sun.

New day dawns, darkness dispelled,
moon leaves the stage, making way for sun.
Sunlight melts into moonlight, heat becomes cool,
Yin embraces yang, equilibrium restored.

Ruth Mawdsley

Weeping willow

Majestic, mighty, oozing strength and power,
green tendrils softly swirling, encircling,
reaching low to meet the grass and earth,
watching, listening, absorbing the world.

Wise old tree, share with me your knowledge,
provide me with strength, let me lean on you.
Wrap around me your tender branches,
and allow me to weep in your embrace.

Let me share your roots, grounding my feet
into the soil, but hiding me away.
Sunlight filters through like fingers of hope,
telling me all will soon be repaired.

Be my sanctuary, where I escape from care,
a constant protector from life's sorrow.
With arms about your knotted, sturdy girth,
sap, like balm, calms my troubled mind.

You have weathered many storms, like me,
and here you are, still strong and proud,
not defeated by the fiercest gales,
resilient, solid, standing up to the world.

From you I receive peace and tranquillity,
strength to carry on from day to day.
Together we will survive a while longer.
Thank you, my beautiful willow tree.

Ruth Mawdsley

Autumn days

Leaves morphing from green to gold,
vermillion, bronze, mahogany.
Twirling, waltzing, floating, lying.
Autumn's colour festival parade,
trees competing for the finest show.

Branches shiver, grey, forlorn,
sad to lose their emerald cloak.
Squirrels busy packing winter store,
hedgehogs scuttle to winter bed,
scent of bonfires drifts on breeze.

Sun lowering, last rays of warmth,
delivering her summer's swansong.
Ethereal mists, dew sparkling grass,
richly aromatic spice-box of earth,
summer blooms take their final bow.

Thoughts turn to chestnuts, cosy fires,
hot chocolate, marshmallows toasted,
country walks gathering nature's jewels.
Blackberry jam, apple crumble, soothing
a gradual transition to winter's chill.

Ruth Mawdsley

Stag night

Air frigid in the car.
A boy, a man, each
in their own generational worlds.
Silver ribbon snakes ahead.
Rounding the bend...

Shockwave.

Squealing brakes,
man and boy thrown into
the same space.

A stag, chin raised, breath silvered.
Time motionless.

Unhurried the beast barks,
muscles ripple into the wood.
Man and boy share the journey home.

Jacky Kennedy

Nightscape

Silver light makes a crinkled path over the sea,
gives a pale edge to smudges of cloud.
Sand, dry and cold under my feet,
takes on a grey sheen, resting
while holiday makers dream.
Incoming tide creeps up the beach
cleansing, smoothing and leaving
sea jewels of milky glass.
Arcing across the bay the moon
leaves shadows under the pier,
glances along a line of beach huts
and fades into growing light

Jacky Kennedy

Good day

When walking down the street,
I don't know who I'll meet,
but I'll say, 'hello!'
to all I know, or don't.
I'll make sure that
I greet them all;
short or tall, large or small,
black, brown or white, 'cos I won't fight,
with any of them.
They're my kin, fat or thin
young or old, shy or bold
gay, trans or straight.

I might be late
but I'm happy to stay,
pass the time of day,
give them a smile,
spend a while,
asking this, asking that,
'How's your mother?'
'How's your cat?'

They may be a druggie,
sober or drunk.
They may be a hippy, new age or punk,
but in the end,
we all need a friend,
and I might be,
the only person they see
..........all....... day,
and life can be lonely.

Janet Blackburn

Voice

When she found her voice
she stood up for herself.
She slung him out,
became one of ‘those feminists’.
She went back to college,
got herself an education,
got herself a career.
Her voice had been hushed,
by the conventions of marriage;
drowned out by the demands of children,
muffled by the washing machine,
distorted by the vacuum cleaner.
Then, one day,
unexpected,
her voice burst out,
with a loud shout,
and told her,
who she was
rather than who she should be.

Janet Blackburn

Newt

her abdomen is full
so she must find a mate
the thought fills her with dread
it will be her first date

there is a male she likes
he has a lovely smile
perhaps he is the one
to make her eggs fertile

the two of them meet up
and go down to the pond
she knows he is the one
with whom to form the bond

he strokes her abdomen
which gives her much pleasure
her eggs start popping out
he supplies his measure

she hides the fertile eggs
safe in a leafy patch
where some weeks later on
they will begin to hatch

but then he just swims off
to fulfil his male need
this makes her furious
that elsewhere he spreads seed

if this were not enough
the eggs get washed away
in one almighty storm
that poured all night and day

she now is so depressed
she wants to end it all
so stays out in the sun
the bird of prey will call

Tony Hargreaves

Seeing is believing

I see a glowing star
but do I know it's there?
It's all down to belief;
my star could be nowhere.

This tiny speck of light
into my eye has sped
so now it's part of me
on retina absorbed.

What distance has it come?
I know light travels fast,
but over vast distance
some aeons may have passed.

This means my shining star
may long ago have died.
Till then it gave out light
that now has just arrived.

My contact with the past
is such a strange idea.
But it is a real fact,
the past is with me here.

Tony Hargreaves

Comfort food

The house waits, alert, as I turn the key,
'I'm here, I'm home, it's only me,' I call.
The house is strangely quiet now,
greets me with a lukewarm sigh.
The house that once created warmth within
waits expectantly for children's laughter.
But only echoes of the past remain,
as it waits for my daughter to come in.

I enter defiantly with my shopping,
drop my bags on the kitchen floor.
I find a proper place for everything;
frozen food in freezer, in the fridge a big meringue.

The doorbell rings, in walks my son
bringing fish and chips with salt and vinegar on.

Eileen Chilvers

Tolson Museum

When I read the newspaper headline:
'Tolson Museum to close in Council cut backs,'
I felt a sense of loss.
At the start of the war, it was a family home.

I saw a large, handsome, Yorkshire stone house
with a huge wooden door, where a telegram
was delivered in the First World War.

The husband opened the envelope; the message read,
'Your son is missing, presumed dead'.
His wife stood still, a knife of pain paralysed her brain.
'Missing, not dead', she repeated again
and again, 'Not dead. Not dead.'

They stood a while. No tears were shed.
'He will be found!' the parents said.
He was, the telegram from the War Office stated.
Their son had fallen on the first day of the Battle of the Somme
where he had lain, unfound for nine months, 'killed in action'.
Frosty fog of desolation seeped through father and mother;
silent tears clung to corners once filled with children's laughter.

The war was drawing to a close, man and wife stood
in the doorway of their big beautiful home when the
telegram came.
They read, their youngest son, not yet twenty one, had been found
dead, on a battle ground, in France.
Two sons now buried abroad.

Turning, as automata,
the parents went inside the house, no longer home.
Hope gone.

Eileen Chilvers

Note: the house was then gifted to the people of Huddersfield, and has its tale to tell of war, of hell waged on foreign soil and personal tragedy. It latterly became a museum and is part of my personal history and the history of Huddersfield.

Almost you

You still sit with style,
leg crossed, ankle flexed, foot pointed.
Silver hair swept up, chic... almost.
Faded beauty lies softly beneath lined and wrinkled skin.
'More tea?' you ask... again.
I smile and decline
with another breezy 'no',
sounding as if it's the first... almost.
Then the ritual.
Photo passed to outstretched hand,
like a key in a lock,
with one turn the memory ignites.

'I'm eighteen... almost.'
Face, half turned, eyes bright
with rememberings, light up.
Past and present collide for one magical moment.
Then, like falling leaves,
memories quietly drift away.
True beauty lies softly beneath
lined and wrinkled paper.
A glimpse of you... almost.

Jane Wilson

Life...

It happens when you are not looking
but in front of your eyes,
this thing called life.

Seconds, minutes, hours
turn into years.

The past, a vastness
of moments encapsulated
into one feeling
so overwhelming
there is no air,
lungs collapse with the
sheer awe of a life
lived and the passing of time...

Breathe...
Inhale... slowly.
Dare to unfold the map of memories
dissolved into matter,
now released.

Your light will forever travel
through the universe
to infinite wordless places.

Reach out, beyond the sea of stars
for that small hand.
Hold it tight...
All will be well.

Jane Wilson

Art and science

I was speaking to my daughter
of the properties of water –
the flow, the singing brooks
reflections on a placid mere
the inspiration of a tear
how it differs from the rocks.

No Dad, she said, *rocks too can flow*
erupt and spew and turn to gas
when subject to sufficient mass -
just watch the molten lava flow
from this Icelandic volcano.

So
it's not important what it is
what matters is how hot it is.

Andrew Shephard

Paddling pool on Ilkley Moor

Turn a corner down decades
to revisit boyhood heaven.
Take a turn around the tarn,
see women walking arm in arm
under lampposts,
me trailing, aged six or seven.

And here, remembered right,
summer sun equally bright,
a spring fed paddling pool
once boiling with children,
now undisturbed brown water
quietly shrunk to grown-up scale.

Remembered for the red cloud
of blood building about my leg,
glass shard unseen,
the cottage hospital,
foot bandaged thick and tight.
No stitches –
a foreign body, a slither
could be deep inside.

Remembered for the baby sister's
rattling pushchair
commandeered.
For the days the toddler walked
while I was pushed.
She complained. I sneered.

Andrew Shephard

Colours of the wind

Nondescript,
but sometimes the dull grey of stone
with its hammerhead pounding in my face.

At times a quieter tone. With silver whispers
as it rustles blossoms on a lilac tree,
or stirs grasses on the hills.

A soft touch of pink as it creates ripples
on a sandy beach
making the waves to curve.

In its strength a purple edge
that creates havoc on mountains, swells rivers
topples trees,

and golden when children fly their kites,
and laughter bounces across
the spectrum of the sky.

Doris Corti

Being here

To glimpse Venice along the waterways
by riverboat or gondola,
is to clutch at fairytales;

it hurtles magic at every curve,
those geraniums, bursting red from pots,
are delightful exclamation marks

and music from open windows
enchants along the winding way,
beneath balustrades of wrought iron filigree.

Slivers of stone steps from huge front doors
descend to alleyways and boats. Voices vibrate
under arches criss-crossing street to street

where children play, and old ladies sit
in sheltered spots, slicing tomatoes and fruit
to idle hours away.

Sunlight weaves patterns on mellow walls,
water lap-laps on sides of boats,
splashes round the wooden props;

hubbub of sounds, voices, melodies
and church clock chimes. Lazy as a lizard
I relax, Venice is too real to photograph.

Doris Corti

Old love

Threads of shared sepia memories
bind us together.
We share painful moments
in our arthritic haze.

We move in synchronised slowness
watching each other as age steals its price
of stiffening limbs and bent backs

We are threaded in an uncertain
longevity,
knowing each one will leave the other.

We do not speak of this as we sit,
our gnarled fingers entwined,
enjoying autumn leaves
falling.

Jackie Darnbrough

The sadness

It is my sadness I carry.
I own it.
Creeping slowly
it follows to stain my day.
Drops of silent loss
spill into screwed-up tissues.

Yet moments of soothing banality
intrude,
darkness fades
into a mist.
I dance with my demons,
trample on pain,
seduce sadness away.

Jackie Darnbrough

Water stones

Smooth shaped pebbles crafted by sea;
fine poetry
on Stanza Stones,
perfectly honed

with the element of water
washing over
Rain, Puddle, Snow,
metaphors flow;

verses organically formed
as words eat stone,
carve a future
to hold water.

Visitor

A white dove settles
at the place where you rest now;
you would be grateful
to this earthly creature for
a sparkle of life in death.

Anne Broadbent

Three haiku

When the music plays
the fire within reignites.
Nothing else matters.

My soul is searching
endless questions in my mind.
Where are the answers?

My heart is pleading.
How to end war and find peace?
Who has the answer?

Gillian McHugh

The storm

Heat had been rising all day.
His shirt stuck to his back,
colour rose in her cheeks.
                                        It broke.

Fork lightening flashed round the room.
Deep rumbling was immediate
rattling the light fitting.

A second's pause, another flash,
thunder overlapped the electric air.
The light bulb, incandescent,
                                        exploded.

In thick half light
he removed the bayonet.
Blood on her blouse
where he'd sliced his hand.

She helped plaster the wound,
lit a candle, opened a bottle.
Red wine lit a path to the bedroom.

Jacky Kennedy

Wild boy (a rescue dog)

I wanted to teach you to play,
you taught me you weren't that kind of dog.
I wanted to teach you the dog trainer's rules,
you taught me rules had no place with you.
Survival is key.
I wanted to teach you to trust,
you taught me patience. Big time.
And over time,
a lot,
we have learnt to live together.
But wildness is imprinted on your soul.
You'll always be that wild boy
running through the trees for the sheer joy of it.

Jacky Kennedy

Fear of change

I gave her the money,
and waited for the change.
I didn't want too much change
or too little change,
as that would have engaged us
in conversation; a debate,
maybe unpleasantness.
I wanted enough change,
the right change
so I could say,
'Thank you'
and 'Goodbye.'

Janet Blackburn

Courage of ordinary people.

It is the woman who shaves her head,
even before the first chemotherapy.
The old man who still smiles philosophically
as he cares for his beloved wife,
whilst her mind unravels.
The child who remains joyful at finishing the race
even though they are last.

The girl, who quietly challenges racism, in the bus queue.
The boy who comes out loud and proud,
to all his macho mates and disapproving parents.
The Mum and Dad, who although crying inside
stay strong, as they hold hands with their dying child.

Tireless volunteers, who fearlessly face danger
to support a stranger, through manmade mayhem
or natural disaster,
with no thought of thanks.
Their names unknown.

It is the extraordinary resilience of ordinary people,
facing life's challenges with fortitude and dignity,
who carry on relentlessly.
When asked they modestly reply
'It's what anyone would do, isn't it?'

If our trial comes, however big or small,
we can but hope to find such courage in our hearts.

Janet Blackburn

We watch the damselfly

We love her slender abdomen
dressed in metallic green
with small black dots just like sequins.
She is the beauty queen.

Her wings are thin transparent film,
so we can see inside
and admire a network of veins
that make her wings spread wide.

We might think they are delicate
but they are stiff and strong
and deliver lots of power
for her to speed along.

One other asset is her eyes:
large domes upon her head.
Each one can see at wide angles
and is a darkish red.

They warn her of approaching threat;
they see the slightest stir.
So if we try to get up close
she's up and in the air.

Of all the insects that we watch,
for colour shape and size,
our damselfly beats all the rest.
So she deserves first prize.

Tony Hargreaves

Celtic River Calder

Sooted mills, snickets, back-to-backs.
Chaos crammed into a valley's groin.
Industry's muscle, now master.

Locals need the bread so do the graft.
Clogs clatter up ginnels to terraces
clinging to the steep.
Stone steps, worn to saddles
by the grit-grind of steel segs.

Hillside trees charred by brimstone fume,
the rising venom from cauldrons below.
Old oaks grumpy with mutated limbs.
Their genes gnarled by acid smoke.

The Calder, once Celtic river goddess,
long since ceased to spawn sacred salmon.
Her new role: to fill the goit to flush the filth,
send it downstream, out of sight.

Man versus Nature. But, a no-match game.
Her side wins. Man's efforts fall silent.
The sacred salmon returns to spawn.

Tony Hargreaves

Where is my sister?

She cannot understand.
Right hand holds the day,
left hand is far away in a land beyond.
She sits, juggling thoughts.

Stretching to catch one in the air,
to bring it down, she watches
as it falls and rolls out of reach.

Straining slightly, she glimpses a
snippet of a wisp of time.
With hands cupped to catch a dream,
eyes closed, she wishes.

Eileen Chilvers

Thank you for the invitation to your barbecue

Can you guarantee a comfortable seat
and will the food be cooked thoroughly?
I hate half raw burgers, burned sausages,
tough pork chops, and salad wilted in the sun.

You can be so innovative, and I appreciate
that it wasn't altogether your fault when things
went disastrously wrong at your last 'do'.
When all the spoiled food got tipped in the bin!

The fish and chips you sent for were a bit off,
but adding curry sauce saved the day, and
your idea of everyone reading aloud from *The Sun* newspaper
they were wrapped in was brilliant.

Thinking it over, I'll come. Count me in!

Eileen Chilvers

A moment in childhood remembered

They keep telling me I should move on.
'You can't live in the past all the time', they say.
'I was happy in the past all the time', I reply,
voice pitched high. I let out a sigh.

Memories whirr and stir the soul,
to surface where Time stood still.
Dark, biting cold of winter gone,
winter of war not yet begun.

Grimy slush of long lain snow
washed away by cleansing rain.
The air was bright, sun warmed her face;
the child held the precious moment close.

War not yet declared. Call up papers
not yet dropped through letter boxes.
No sound of sirens warning, as it mocks
impending enemy attacks.

Effortlessly, through time and space
she jumped with grace and innocence,
not stopping for breath, connected to Earth.
Warmth seeped deep in all her senses,

soaking her heart with purest joy.
Fleetingly, feeling the knowing of being,
she slowed her skipping, to experience
the moment in Time, treasured forever.

Eileen Chilvers

Five again

In one molecule of a moment
lost and forgotten,
now remembered whole, mind feeling
what was captured,
past and present collide.

Hollow thuds on warm sand,
feet pounding,
carrying me without a care.
Mind giddy with the vastness
of distant horizons.

Sights, sounds, salty smells
surround my senses,
buzzing around my head like
summer bees.

In this haven where the sky
meets the sea
I am five once more and free
in this forever place.

Jane Wilson

Footsteps from the past...

Take a moment ... now.
Breathe.
Surrender.
Deep below our feet,
cloaked in eons of time,
buried in Earth's mantle,
worn paths of ancient souls
still vibrate, unseen but felt.
Rhythms, heel to toe
beat track and treads of longings and losses.
Pounded paths of thoughts and dreams.
Trails of togetherness and walking out alone.
Barefoot engrained with dust and dirt and soil.
Take a moment now.
Breathe.
Surrender.
Step off this sealed earth,
take off your shoes,
plant both feet into the
home from where they came.
Trust.
Make room for this new awakening.

Jane Wilson

Garden bake off

The girl observes a battalion of bees
busy on raspberry canes.
Gooseberries tart, apples and pears undecided
plums hiding, green as leaves
strawberries wait between flower and fruit.
'I'm hungry, Grandad.'

Runner beans compete up poles,
pretty potatoes grow tall, not fat.
Rhubarb's ridiculous leaves
shelter stems too short for crumble.
'Is there anything to eat, Grandad?'

Finches tear seeds from
over-the-top forget-me-nots.
Black singer lords it from gable end,
charming worms to come and play.
Thrush bashes snails on Yorkshire stone.
'But what about us, Grandad?'

She collects pots, sticks and water
makes a feast while crops mature.
Starters, mud soup herbed
with clippings from the lawn.
Mains, pizza of small white stones
topped with compost paste and petals
yellow, blue and white.

'Have you room for dessert, Grandad?'
Log roll, decorative dirt,
recipe secret to those of tender years.

Replete with sunshine,
we stand back to judge the fare.

Andrew Shephard

Happy ending

On my last day I did not fret.
I walked old dog along the lane
enjoyed the breeze with no regret.
On my last day
I ate lunch early on a tray
then spent some cash by internet –
a gift for you, I'm pleased to say.
I studied form and placed a bet
(the three fifteen at Galway Bay)
not knowing I would not collect
on my last day.

Andrew Shephard

Frost

His name is Jack,
he spreads his hand, across
the bleak and barren land;
sprinkles sparkles on the trees
forms icicles in air he breathes.
In pink low sun of winters sky,
etched ferns on glass as he went by:
Ice dusted meadows twinkle bright,
mirrored ponds reflect the light.
A myriad colours glitter, shine
to brighten grey, dull wintertime.
Stealthily, silently he has been
painting this iridescent scene.
His name is Jack

Janet Blackburn

In between

bubbling day dreams
and night wings dark broodings
I lost my way. That beginning - the hesitation
between imagination and reason.

The sense of loss, not quite a grief - that yearning
after elusive words. And that frenzy of nothing formed,
the continual tormenting, an insect twitching
on my arm; that not quite there-ness.

Over the cooking, sorting washing,
packing children's lunch boxes, comes the glimmer
of words, suddenly, almost,

then the negotiating, placing them in order.
Stealing hours from daily routines, clutching
fleeting words as they alight like butterflies,

here and there,
beautiful.

Doris Corti

Meet the Poets

Janet Blackburn

Janet joined the U3A poetry group after retiring from a career working with people. Playing with words, rhyme and rhythm keeps her mind active. She also enjoys and is fascinated by the different ways people express themselves and their feelings through the complex discipline of poetry.

Anne Broadbent

Anne believes the support of the U3A poetry group is an important part of her writing. She was the winner of the Mrs Sunderland Adult Open Poetry Competition 2016, placed in the top twelve poems at Huddersfield Literature Festival 2017, and has a poem in the *Body and Soul* NHS at 70 anthology. Living in the Holme Valley, she is often inspired by its countryside while walking her dog.

Eileen Chilvers

A retired social worker, Eileen joined the U3A poetry group two years ago. She says poetry has not completely taken over her life, but has certainly changed it on many levels. She wishes she had met Doris Corti many years ago.

Doris Corti

Doris's love of poetry began when she was reading poems whilst doing her homework in an air-raid shelter in her garden in London during the Second World War. She has been published, won prizes, run courses and workshops as well as working on the 'Poets in Schools' scheme for eighteen years. As a freelance writer and a Vice President of the Society of Women Writers and Journalists, Doris has written several non-fiction books including a text book *Writing Poetry* which is still the go-to book for poets. Doris wrote the Poetry Home Study Course for *Writers News*, for which she was also a tutor. She now writes a monthly poetry feature for *Writing Magazine*, judges poetry competitions, gives talks and leads the Huddersfield U3A Writing Poetry class.

JACKIE DARNBROUGH

Jackie has written poetry throughout her life. She has been published in *An Anthology of Local Poets* by Huddersfield University. A member of the U3A poetry group for many years, she is also a contributing member of Batley Poets. She enjoys painting pictures with words.

TONY HARGREAVES

Tony Hargreaves is a science writer and writes for magazines and journals. He has also published text books, the latest being about the forensic science of poisons. Now he tries his hand at writing verse. His poems are often published online, and his work has been included in the *Body and Soul* NHS at 70 anthology.

JACKY KENNEDY

Jacky Kennedy has written sporadically since she was a child, usually in the form of short stories, some of which have been published. She was shortlisted in the short story competition in the very first Huddersfield Literary Festival. Poetry is a recent venture and Jacky enjoys creating the essence of an idea in this shortened writing form.

RUTH MAWDSLEY

A retired lecturer in Health and Social Care, with a previous background in care, Ruth enjoys writing, painting, reading and nature. She and her husband moved to Huddersfield in 2017. She has two daughters and two granddaughters, with whom she loves to spend her time.

GILLIAN MCHUGH

Gillian's first love is singing (she is in two choirs), and enjoys the rhythm and rhyme of a good hymn. She joined the U3A poetry group three years ago after meeting Doris Corti in Lindley Library. A nurse for forty years and now retired, Gillian moved from Halifax to Huddersfield in 1969 when she married.

ANDREW SHEPHARD

The publication of work-related magazine articles infected Andrew with an enthusiasm for writing which moved on to fiction and poetry when he gave up full time employment. He has written four novels, the latest of which, *Nellie and Tabs*, is available through Amazon books. His poems appear in *The Yorkshire Writers' Lunch* blog. He lives in Huddersfield with a wife, dog, and garden.

JANE WILSON

Poetry and writing have been a strong thread throughout Jane's life, linking her many creative interests which include mixed media art, philosophy, astronomy and travel. Jane is a staff nurse and the mother of two fabulous daughters. Currently Artist in Residence at the Lawrence Batley Theatre, Jane also has a poem in the *Body and Soul* NHS anthology.

Acknowledgements

A number of the poems in this volume have been published previously including:

Fox in suburbia (Doris Corti) in *Beyond the Skyline* (Assistance of Fenland Arts Small Grants Scheme) and *Avenue of Days* (SCRIPTORA).

Party shoes (Doris Corti) in *Avenue of Days* (SCRIPTORA) and 3rd prize SWWJ's Elizabeth Longford Poetry Competition 2012.

In between (Doris Corti) in *Kingfisher and Other Things* (SCRIPTORA), *Acumen Literary Journal* and *Caduceus* magazine.

A skylark's song (Doris Corti) in *Avenue of Days* (SCRIPTORA), and winner of NAWG Open Poetry competition 2013.

Colours of the wind (Doris Corti) in *Kingfisher and Other Things* (SCRIPTORA), and *Acumen Literary Journal* (guest poem).

Being here (Doris Corti) in *Kingfisher and Other Things* (SCRIPTORA).

Almost you (Jane Wilson) in *Body and Soul* (Otley Word Feast Press).

20309298R00041

Printed in Great Britain
by Amazon